DISCOVERING *Space*

STARS AND GALAXIES

Ian Graham

A⁺

Smart Apple Media

Published by Smart Apple Media
2140 Howard Drive West
North Mankato, MN 56003

Created by Q2A Creative
Series Editor: Honor Head
Designers: Diksha Khatri, Ashita Murgai
Picture Researchers: Lalit Dalal, Jyoti Sachdev

Printed in China

Library of Congress Cataloging-in-Publication Data

Graham, Ian, 1953-
Stars and galaxies / by Ian Graham.
p.cm. — (Discovering space)
Includes index.
ISBN 978-1-59920-073-6
1. Stars—Juvenile literature. 2. Galaxies—Juvenile literature. I. Title.

QB801.7.G73 2007
523.8—dc22   2007007531

First Edition

9 8 7 6 5 4 3 2 1

Contents

The night sky

At night, the sky is full of twinkling points of light. Nearly all of these are stars. Many of them are like our star, the **sun**. The stars look much smaller than the sun because they are so far away.

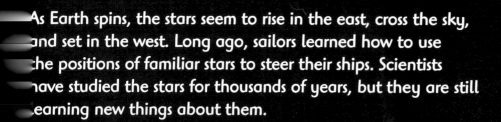

Rising and setting

As Earth spins, the stars seem to rise in the east, cross the sky, and set in the west. Long ago, sailors learned how to use the positions of familiar stars to steer their ships. Scientists have studied the stars for thousands of years, but they are still learning new things about them.

On a clear night, you can see about 2,000 stars in the sky.

When you look at the stars, you are seeing light that has crossed billions of miles of space.

Clusters of stars

Stars are not spread evenly throughout the **universe**. They gather together in giant clusters called galaxies. A **galaxy** contains **billions** of stars traveling through space, held together by **gravity**. Everywhere **astronomers** look in the sky, they find more and more galaxies. There are billions of galaxies, and each galaxy contains billions of stars.

Closest stars

Name of star	Distance from Earth
Sun	0.000016 light-years
Proxima centauri	4.24 light-years
Alpha centauri A	4.35 light-years
Alpha centauri B	4.35 light-years
Barnard's star	5.98 light-years
Wolf 359	7.78 light-years
Lalande 21185	8.26 light-years
Sirius A	8.55 light-years
Sirius B	8.55 light-years
Luyten 726-8A	8.73 light-years

Spotlight on
space

Long distances are usually measured in miles. But the distances between stars are so big that they are measured in units called light-years. A light-year is the distance light travels in one year, or nearly six trillion miles (10 trillion km).

Birth of a star

There was a time when each star that shines in the night sky did not exist. Stars have been forming for billions of years and new stars are still being born. Stars form in a vast cloud of gas and dust, called a **nebula,** that drifts through space. Scientists can see nebulae (more than one nubula) and study the stars being formed in them.

The four biggest stars seen here are still very young—only a few hundred thousand years old.

Gas balls

Inside a nebula, gravity pulls together some of the gas to form thick clumps. These clumps pull more gas into them. The clumps slowly grow bigger and bigger. As each clump grows, the gas at its center is squeezed harder and begins to heat up.

These stars are forming in giant pillars of gas and dust in the Eagle nebula.

New stars are formed in a nebula when a dying star explodes and sends gas rushing into it. Waves of the gas push into the nebula and squeeze parts of it. Then gravity takes over, and the formation of the new stars begins.

New stars are formed in gas clouds such as the Orion nebula.

Star light

Orion nebula facts

Size	30 light-years
Distance from Earth	1,500 light-years away

As a new star grows and heats up, it is hidden inside the nebula in which it formed. Eventually, the center of the new star reaches several million degrees Fahrenheit. Particles of matter smash into each other so hard that they stick together, or fuse, and give off a burst of energy. This is called nuclear fusion, and when it begins, the star starts to give off light.

Star colors

Stars look like identical pinpoints of light, but there are many differences between them. Some are **dwarf stars** no bigger than Earth. Others are supergiants 1,000 times bigger than the sun—and there are even stars that pulse like heartbeats.

The color of heat

The sun is yellow because it is so hot. Its surface temperature is 9,932 °F (5,500 °C). Stars hotter than the sun are white, blue, or violet. Stars cooler than the sun are orange or red.

The Pleiades, or Seven Sisters, is a cluster of young, hot stars.

Star color facts

Color of star	Temperature
Violet	more than 50,000 °F (28,000 °C)
Blue	13,532–50,432 °F (7,500–28,000 °C)
Blue-white	10,832–13,532 °F (6,000–7,500 °C)
White-yellow	9,032–10,832 °F (5,000–6,000 °C)
Orange-red	6,332–9,032 °F (3,500–5,000 °C)
Red	less than 6,332 °F (less than 3,500 °C)

Spotlight on
space

More than half of the stars in the sky are not alone, such as the sun. These stars are actually in pairs, and they orbit around each other. Two stars orbiting each other are called a **binary star**.

Variable stars

Stars that change in brightness are called **variable stars**. Some variable stars grow brighter or dimmer because they are growing or shrinking. Sometimes a star suddenly becomes 10,000 times brighter. This is a **nova**. A nova happens when one star pulls gas off another star. The extra gas piles up on the star and explodes in a dazzling flash.

Mira, in the far-off **constellation** Cetus, was the first variable star to be discovered. These pictures show how its brightness changes.

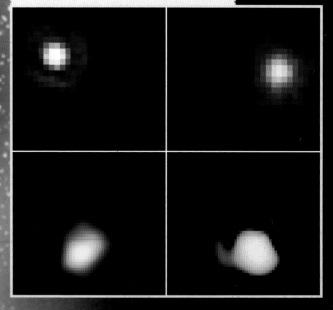

Most of the stars in the night sky are too dim to be seen without a telescope.

Star death

A star may shine for billions of years, but eventually, it will run out of the fuel it needs to keep shining. What happens then depends on how big the star is. It might just fade away, or it might explode into countless pieces.

Star size

Type of star	Size across the middle
The sun	870,000 miles (1.4 million km)
A red giant	up to 1,000 suns
A white dwarf	about the same size as Earth
A neutron star	about 12.5 miles (20 km)

The smallest stars

When a star such as the sun begins to run out of **hydrogen**, it swells to form a huge star called a **red giant**. In time, the star's outer layers of hot gas drift away into space. All that is left behind is a tiny star called a **white dwarf**. A white dwarf is made of matter that is so tightly packed together that just a teaspoonful would weigh 1.1 tons (1 t). White dwarfs cool down and fade until they are completely gone.

A red giant star is red because its outer layers cool down and glow red as the star grows bigger.

This is the shattered remains of a star that exploded in a **supernova** more than 340 years ago.

Spotlight on
space

When the biggest stars explode, they produce one of the strangest objects in the universe—a black hole. When the star's core collapses, its gravity is so strong that **nothing can escape from its pull, not even light.**

Flash, bang, pulse!

Stars much bigger than the sun collapse so powerfully that they are broken into tiny pieces in a dazzling explosion called a supernova. All that is left is a small spinning core called a **neutron star**, which sends out narrow beams of radio waves. If the radio waves sweep past Earth, the neutron star seems to have a throbbing pulse. This is called a pulsating star, or **pulsar.**

A supernova blasts stardust in all directions.

Constellations

For thousands of years, people who studied the stars divided them into groups called constellations. Today, astronomers still use constellations as a map to find their way around the sky.

Naming the constellations

Many of the constellations astronomers know today were named thousands of years ago by astronomers in the Middle East and ancient Greece. When these first astronomers saw a group of stars that looked like an animal or a person or creature from mythology, they named the stars after it.

Lines drawn around constellations of stars show how they look like their name. This is Capricorn, the "goat."

Zodiac constellation names

Name		Shape
Aries	▶	ram
Taurus	▶	bull
Gemini	▶	twins
Cancer	▶	crab
Leo	▶	lion
Virgo	▶	girl
Libra	▶	scales
Scorpio	▶	scorpion
Sagittarius	▶	archer
Capricorn	▶	goat
Aquarius	▶	water bearer
Pisces	▶	fish

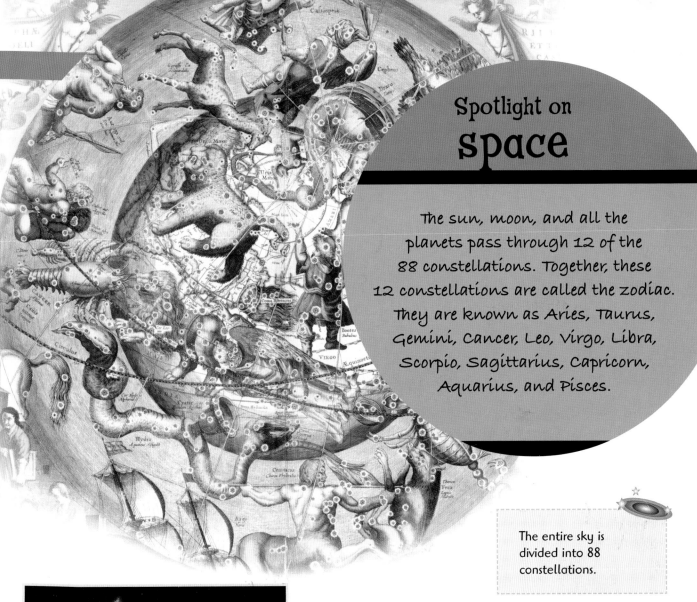

Spotlight on
space

The sun, moon, and all the planets pass through 12 of the 88 constellations. Together, these 12 constellations are called the zodiac. They are known as Aries, Taurus, Gemini, Cancer, Leo, Virgo, Libra, Scorpio, Sagittarius, Capricorn, Aquarius, and Pisces.

The entire sky is divided into 88 constellations.

Ancient constellations

The stars in a constellation are not usually close together. Some of them are much farther away from Earth than other stars in the same constellation. They appear to be close together when we look into the night sky, but they are light-years apart.

The constellation Orion is named after the great hunter from the myths of ancient Greece.

Galaxies

Galaxies are huge collections of stars moving through space. They are many different shapes and sizes. The smallest galaxies may contain just a few million stars. The biggest have hundreds of billions of stars.

Spinning in space

The stars in a galaxy are pulled toward each other, but they do not fall into the center of the galaxy because the whole galaxy is spinning. The spinning galaxy is pulling the stars apart. This is balanced by gravity, which is pulling the stars together.

Andromeda facts

Size	▶	160,000 light-years wide
Number of stars	▶	400 billion
Distance from Earth	▶	2.4 million light-years

Galaxies sometimes crash into each other, producing long tails and swirls of stars and gas.

The Andromeda galaxy is a giant spiral galaxy.

Interesting shapes

e galaxies are much brighter than expect them to be. These are called sars. Scientists think a quasar's a light is given off by stars and gas, just before they fall into a gigantic black hole at the center of the galaxy.

Most galaxies have an elliptical shape that is similar to the shape of a football. Some galaxies are spirals. They have long swirls of stars and gas that curl away from a ball of stars in the middle. More than one-third of all galaxies have no definite shape. These are called irregular galaxies.

Some spiral galaxies have a line of stars, dust, and gas across the middle.

The Milky Way

Earth is part of a galaxy called the Milky Way. If we could look at our galaxy from above, we would see that the Milky Way is a spiral galaxy. It contains about 200 billion stars.

Old and young

The stars in the central bulge—in the middle of the Milky Way—are older than the stars in the spiral arms. The arms contain a lot of gas and dust where new stars are still forming. Earth is in one of the galaxy's spiral arms.

Milky Way facts	
Size	up to 100,000 light-years wide
Central bulge	15,000 light-years wide and 6,000 light-years deep
Number of stars	about 200 billion

Spiral arms

Central bulge

Our galaxy, called the Milky Way, is a spiral galaxy.

The center of our galaxy is a mystery, hidden behind clouds of dust. Scientists think there is a massive black hole there. More than two million suns may have fallen into it. But don't worry, there is no danger of Earth falling in!

The Local Group

Our galaxy is one of a cluster of galaxies that travel through space together called the Local Group. There are about 40 galaxies in the Local Group. Clusters of galaxies sometimes combine with other clusters to form a supercluster. The Local Group belongs to a supercluster called the Local Supercluster.

The center of the Milky Way may look like this, with stars and gas shining brightly as they spiral into a black hole.

Space clouds

Galaxies contain vast clouds of gas and dust called nebulae. New stars are made in some nebulae. Other nebulae are the remains of old, dying, or dead stars.

Light and dark

Some nebulae are bright and easy to see. They are lit up by nearby stars. Other nebulae are surrounded by dust, so they are darker and harder to see. They look like a dark shadow if there is a bigger, brighter nebula behind them.

Horsehead nebula facts

Distance from Earth	▶	1,600 light-years
Size	▶	3.5 light-years wide
Location	▶	Orion constellation

This dusty, dark nebula is called the Horsehead nebula because of its shape.

Fuzzy planets or stars?

More than 200 years ago, astronomers discovered tiny, fuzzy disks of light in the sky. Through a telescope, they looked like planets, so they were called planetary nebulae. Today, scientists know that these disks have nothing to do with planets—they are old stars that have blown a lot of their gas out into space.

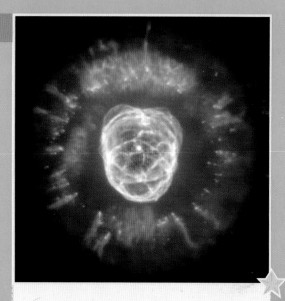

This planetary nebula is called the Eskimo nebula because it looks like a face inside a furry hood.

Spotlight on
space

The gas and dust in a nebula are scattered throughout space. All of the gas and dust from an area 475 miles (764 km) long, 475 miles (764 km) wide, and 475 miles (764 km) high, would weigh only one pound (0.45 kg)!

All nebula are mostly made of hydrogen.

The big bang

Did the universe have a beginning, or has it been here forever? Scientists had different ideas about this in the past. Today, most scientists think the universe began nearly 14 billion years ago in a gigantic explosion called the **big bang**.

Cooling down

Moments after the big bang, the temperature of the universe was about 1.8 billion °F (1 billion °C). The universe has been cooling down ever since. A satellite called *COBE* (the *Cosmic Background Explorer*) made a map of the heat created by the big bang.

COBE mission

Launched	▶	1989
Orbit	▶	559 miles (900 km) above the ground
Length of mission	▶	4 years
Mission ended	▶	1993

The *COBE* satellite **scanned** the entire sky every six months

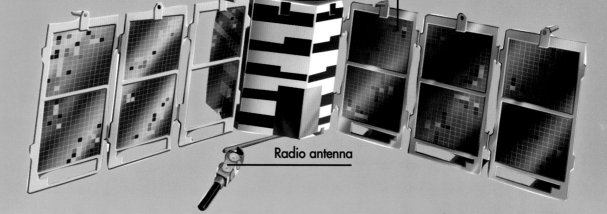

Heat shield protects instruments

Solar panels produce electricity

Radio antenna

Spotlight on
space

Scientists believe that within a few seconds of the big bang, the first particles of matter began to form. A few hundred thousand years later, the first stars lit up the young universe.

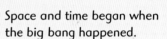

Space and time began when the big bang happened.

COBE's heat map of the big bang's echo shows the ripples that would become the first galaxies.

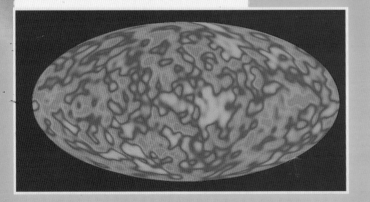

Flying apart

The universe has been growing ever since the big bang. Scientists thought gravity was acting like a brake and slowing down this growth. They even thought that gravity might stop the universe from growing and cause it to collapse in something called the "big crunch." However, astronomers have discovered that the galaxies are flying apart faster and faster, but no one understands why.

Star gazing

The stars and galaxies are so far away that we cannot visit them or send space probes to explore them. Scientists study them by using telescopes on Earth. Telescopes in space collect light and other energy that stars and galaxies give off.

Twinkle, twinkle

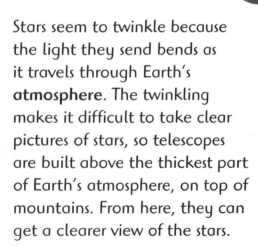

Stars seem to twinkle because the light they send bends as it travels through Earth's **atmosphere**. The twinkling makes it difficult to take clear pictures of stars, so telescopes are built above the thickest part of Earth's atmosphere, on top of mountains. From here, they can get a clearer view of the stars.

Modern astronomical telescopes have a huge, curved mirror to collect starlight.

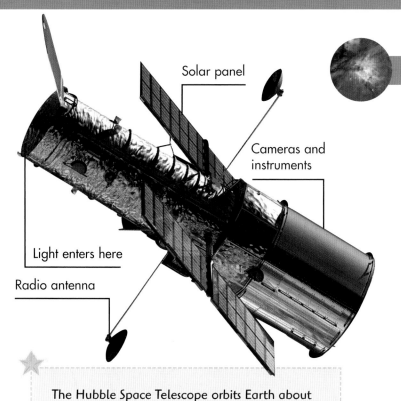

Solar panel

Cameras and instruments

Light enters here

Radio antenna

The Hubble Space Telescope orbits Earth about 373 miles (600 km) above the ground.

The telescopes of the Mauna Kea **Observatory** in Hawaii are built on top of a sleeping volcano.

Space telescopes

Earth's atmosphere blocks some of the energy given off by stars. Telescopes on Earth cannot receive this energy, but telescopes in space are able to study all of the energy given off by stars and galaxies. Some space telescopes produce pictures from invisible **ultraviolet rays**. Others receive **infrared rays**, or X-rays. The Hubble Space Telescope produces pictures from light.

Hubble Space Telescope facts

Length	▷	43 feet (13 m)
Diameter	▷	up to 14 feet (4.2 m)
Weight	▷	12.8 tons (11.6 t)
Primary mirror	▷	7.9 feet (2.4 m) wide

Solar systems

The sun is not the only star with planets orbiting it. There are planets orbiting other stars—these are called **extrasolar planets** or exoplanets. Exoplanets are hard to find because they are so far away, hidden in the bright light of the stars.

Alien giants

About 200 exoplanets have been found. Most of them are huge planets, even bigger than the giant of our **solar system**, Jupiter. Scientists believe there are also exoplanets as small as Earth.

This is what a giant exoplanet orbiting a small star 200 light-years from Earth might look like.

Exoplanet facts

First exoplanet found	1992
Closest exoplanet	63 light-years away
Farthest exoplanet	21,500 light-years away
Oldest exoplanet	13 billion years old

Finding planets

Exoplanets are hard to see, but the pull of their gravity as they orbit a star can also make the star move. So a wobbling star may have planets. If a planet moves in front of a star, the light from the star will look less bright. Sometimes dust around a star will show if it has a planet—the planet's gravity can change the shape of the dust cloud around the star.

The Terrestrial Planet Finder is an instrument that will search for Earth-sized planets orbiting other stars.

Kepler looks for dips in starlight caused by planets.

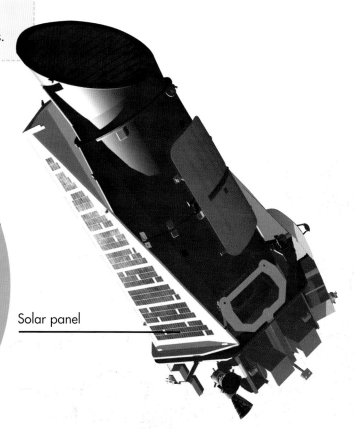

Solar panel

Spotlight on space

A spacecraft called *Kepler* will be launched in 2008 to search for planets the same size as Earth. Its 37.4-inch (95 cm) telescope will watch 100,000 stars—all at the same time—for any sign that small planets are orbiting them.

Searching for aliens

People have wondered for thousands of years if we are alone in the universe. So far, we have not found life on any other planet. But some scientists are studying stars for signs of intelligent beings that might live on the planets orbiting the stars.

Is anybody out there?

Looking for intelligent beings in space is called the Search For Extraterrestrial Intelligence (SETI). SETI scientists use radio telescopes to try to pick up radio signals from other forms of life in space.

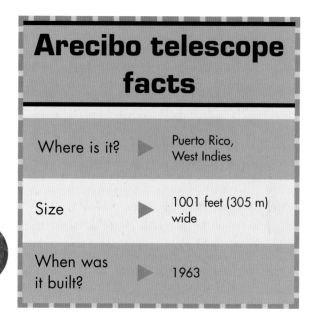

Arecibo telescope facts

Where is it?	▶	Puerto Rico, West Indies
Size	▶	1001 feet (305 m) wide
When was it built?	▶	1963

The Arecibo radio telescope is used to listen for possible alien radio messages.

This is an artist's idea of what an alien spacecraft might look like.

Help look for aliens

SETI scientists started a project that anyone with a computer can help with. The "SETI@home" project asks people to look for radio signals from space. Five million home computers in 200 countries around the world are helping scientists search for alien, or extraterrestrial, life.

Spotlight on
space

In 1977, SETI scientists received a radio signal from space. One scientist wrote "Wow!" on the page where the signal was recorded. This radio signal is still known as the Wow! signal. No one knows if it was really from aliens.

SETI scientists study results from the Arecibo radio telescope.

Time line

140 B.C.
The Greek astronomer Hipparchus produced the first known star catalog, with accurate positions for about 800 stars.

ca. A.D. 950
The Persian astronomer 'Abd al-Rahman al-Sufi created a star catalog. He is also the first person known to have seen the two brightest galaxies that can be seen without a telescope—the Andromeda galaxy and the Large Magellanic Cloud.

1006
A brilliant supernova is seen in a constellation called Lupus.

1054
A brilliant supernova appears in the constellation Taurus. The remains of the star that blew itself apart are still visible today as the Crab nebula

1572
A supernova explodes in the constellation Cassiopeia.

1612
The Orion nebula is discovered.

1802
The German-born astronomer William Herschel discovers binary stars.

1834
Astronomers discover that the star Sirius moves slightly and suggest that there must be another star orbiting it.

1838
John Herschel, the son of William Herschel, makes the first detailed survey of the far southern stars, while he is in southern Africa.

1845
Irish astronomer Lord Rosse builds the world's biggest telescope at Birr Castle in Ireland.

1863
Astronomers divide stars into different types according to their colors and temperatures.

1864
Astronomers discover that nebulae are made of gas.

1885
A supernova is seen in the Andromeda galaxy.

1901
A brilliant supernova is seen in the Perseus constellation.

1918
Astronomers calculate the size of the Milky Way.

1923
American astronomer Edwin Hubble proves that the galaxies are outside the Milky Way.

1931
American scientist Karl Jansky discovers radio waves coming from space.

1937
American astronomer Grote Reber builds the first radio telescope.

1938
Scientists begin to discover what makes stars shine.

1955
The world's biggest radio telescope is built at Jodrell Bank in the United Kingdom.

1960
Construction of the Arecibo radio telescope begins on the island of Puerto Rico.

1963
The first quasars are discovered.

1967
British scientist Jocelyn Bell-Burnell discovers the first pulsar.

1974
A radio message is beamed from the Arecibo radio dish in the direction of a cluster of stars that is 25,000 light-years away—it will take 25,000 years to get there. If any aliens receive it, a reply from them will take another 25,000 years to return to Earth.

1977
Scientists receive a radio signal that might have been sent by aliens.

1978
The *Einstein X-ray Observatory* is launched into space.

The *International Ultraviolet Explorer* satellite is launched.

1983
The *Infrared Astronomical Satellite (IRAS)* is launched.

1990
The Hubble Space Telescope is launched.

The *ROSAT X-ray* satellite is launched.

1991
The *Compton Gamma Ray Observatory* is launched into space to study distant explosions in space called gamma ray bursts.

1995
The *Infrared Space Observatory* is launched.

1996
The *Beppo-Sax X-ray* satellite is launched.

1999
The Chandra X-ray Telescope and Newton X-ray Telescope are launched to study objects in space, including pulsars and black holes.

2003
The Spitzer Infrared Space Telescope is launched to study cool objects in space, including cool stars, exoplanets, and giant cool clouds of gas and dust.

2005
The first photograph is taken of a planet orbiting another star.

2008
Launch of the *Kepler* spacecraft to search for Earth-sized planets orbiting other stars.

2011
Launch of the James Webb Space Telescope.

Glossary

astronomers Scientists who study astronomy.

atmosphere The gas around a planet or moon. Earth's atmosphere is made of air.

big bang The explosion that brought the universe into being nearly 14 billion years ago.

black hole An object in space with a pull of gravity so strong that not even light can escape from it.

constellation One of 88 groups of stars.

dwarf stars Small stars such as the sun.

extrasolar planets Planets orbiting a star that is not the sun. Also called exoplanets.

galaxy A collection of stars moving through space, held together by their pull of gravity.

gravity An invisible force that pulls things toward each other. Earth's gravity pulls us down onto the ground. The sun's gravity holds the planets in their orbits.

hydrogen A colorless gas. Stars are mostly made of hydrogen.

infrared rays Energy waves that are longer than red light.

light-years Units of measurement. One light-year is the distance light travels in one year, or nearly 6 trillion miles (10 trillion km).

mythology A collection of myths or stories usually about superhuman beings and their adventures.

nebulae Clouds of gas and dust in space.

neutron star The smallest type of star; the remains of a huge star that has exploded. It is called a neutron star because it is made of particles of matter called neutrons.

nova A sudden burst of energy that makes a star hundreds of thousands of times brighter for a short time.

observatory A building or buildings with telescopes for studying objects in the universe.

orbit To travel around the sun, a moon, or a planet.

planets Huge objects in orbit around a star.

pulsar A spinning neutron star producing beams of radio waves that sweep past Earth, so the star appears to have a throbbing pulse.

quasar The dazzling, bright center of a distant galaxy, probably caused by stars and gas heating up before they fall into a black hole.

red giant A star that has swelled and turned red because it has run out of hydrogen.

scanned Observed or studied closely.

solar system The sun, planets, moons, and everything else that orbit the sun, traveling through space together.

sun Earth's star, the star at the center of the solar system.

supernova A giant explosion that blows a massive star apart.

ultraviolet rays Invisible rays that come from the sun. These "UV" rays can burn our skin.

universe All of space, matter, and energy, and everything else that exists.

variable stars Stars that can be brighter or darker.

white dwarf A star made of as much matter as the sun, but that is as small as Earth. A white dwarf is formed when a star similar to the sun reaches the end of its life.

zodiac The 12 constellations that the sun, moon, and all the planets pass through.

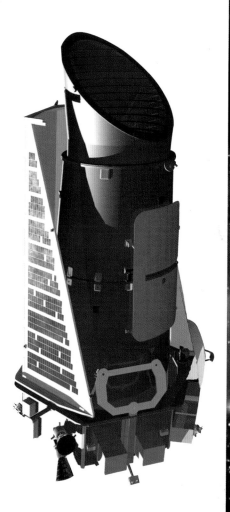

Index

WEB SITES

http://www-spof.gsfc.nasa.gov/stargaze/Ssky.htm

http://spaceplace.nasa.gov/en/kids/cs_space.shtml

http://www.kidsastronomy.com/galaxys.htm

http://coolcosmos.ipac.caltech.edu/cosmic_kids/AskKids/index.shtml

http://www.esa.int/esaKIDSen/Starsandgalaxies.html

http://www.space.kids.us/themilkyway.html